The State of the Nation

A Christian Approach to Britain's Economic Crisis

David L. Edwards
Canon of Westminster

Church H[illegible] Office
[illegible]ndon SW1P 3NZ

ISBN 0 7151 6546 1

Published for the General Synod Board for Social Responsibility
by the Church Information Office

Printed by The Ludo Press Ltd., London SW18 3DG

FOREWORD
by
the Lord Bishop of Leicester

In asking Canon David Edwards to write the present pamphlet, the Board for Social Responsibility had two objects in view. They believed it would provide a useful starting-point for debate in the General Synod on our nation's present economic troubles. They are making it generally available because they consider that it will also help many people in the country to understand the nature of the crisis and explore possible ways forward.

Those who read it will recognise that it gives only one person's point of view, but the author, although not a professional politician, industrialist or economist, has a powerful and well-equipped mind trained in the weighing of historical evidence, and is in constant touch with politicians of every hue. It further represents the outcome of wide consultation, including discussion with members of the Board's Industrial Committee. Canon Edwards shows in the early parts of his paper his command of the theological and moral aspects of the whole problem, and I am very grateful for his clear analysis of Britain's present troubles.

I gladly commend it as a contribution to future serious discussion, although Canon Edwards would be the first to disclaim any idea that it represents an official Church of England view on the many disputed issues raised in its pages.

RONALD LEICESTER

Chairman of the Board for Social Responsibility

January 1976

CONTENTS

I THE CHURCH'S CONTRIBUTION

1. Since any mixture of religion and politics is liable to produce confusion or worse, it will in the end save time (and perhaps more) if we begin with a little theology.

2. We should not look for specifically Christian economics or politics, since no recipe for national prosperity is proclaimed in the Christian Gospel. Jesus grew up in a Palestine which suffered from many economic ills. In effect it was a Roman colony. Its methods of sowing, weed-control and reaping were all primitive. Many landowners were absentees, and the managers they installed dishonest. Many men were unemployed, and almost all women condemned to drudgery. Many people were heavily in debt. Judges did not care about the poor. The easiest way to make a fortune was to buy a pearl for the luxury market, if one was not so lucky as to acquire a property worth more than its seller thought. Although there was an elementary banking system, all classes tended to keep their assets in forms subject to rust, moth, burglary and loss, and to spend them on frivolities from costly perfume to village wedding feasts. But Jesus never denounced Roman soldiers or officials. On the contrary, he admired their discipline and he urged collaboration with them (turning the other cheek and going the second mile). And no explicit attack on the economically disastrous customs of his time is recorded. On the contrary, he used these customs without comment to illustrate his teaching. He refused to arbitrate in a financial dispute. The inner circle of his disciples included one who had been an employee in the grinding and corrupt taxation system, alongside one who had been a freedom fighter – living proof that his message transcended economic and political interests. In his period of retreat after his baptism he was tempted to concentrate on economic and political objectives, feeding the hungry and restoring Israel to its pride as one of the kingdoms of the world; and throughout his public ministry he was surrounded by the sick as clamouring reminders of the people's need of physical and psychological medicine. Yet he always concentrated on prayer, on preaching and on training his

disciples. He became a poor man, without job, home or family, and his great sympathy with the poor is evident in many places in the records of his life and teaching. But so far from devoting himself to agitation on behalf of the poor, he congratulated them. He taught them they had a better chance than the rich of entering the Kingdom of God, the central theme of his message and life. He seems to have accepted the inevitability of the worldly situation of Lazarus, although he was glad to think that the roles of the beggar and the glutton would be reversed in the life to come.

3. The non-economic and non-political content of the apostolic Gospel is illustrated by the fact that the greatest theologians of the first century, Paul and John, refrained from demanding the end of imperialism or the abolition of slavery or the liberation of women. Since the apostles' days the Gospel has been believed sincerely by people whose economic positions and political outlooks have ranged from a Byzantine emperor's to a New England farmer's. In the twentieth century Christians have varied from Camilo Torres the guerilla-priest to General Franco. In our own country and time, among those deeply influenced by the Gospel and by Christian worship are to be found adherents of all the political parties. Dr Stephen Mayor has written a history of *The Churches and the Labour Movement* (1967); but possibly a history of 'the Tory Party at prayer' would be too large to fit into one book. This record of disagreement between Christians about economics or politics shows that what unites them lies at another level; and the whole story of the Christian centuries shows how the best thing that any Church can do for any people at any time is to be powerful in faith, hope and love.

4. It is therefore understandable that a devout Anglican layman such as Mr Enoch Powell in *No Easy Answers* (1973, p.116) should quote with scorn an example of an ecclesiastical conference intruding into the realm of Caesar. The then Bishop of Carlisle commended in *The Times* in 1970 a resolution passed in his diocese calling on the Government 'to take the lead to integrate public and private investment so that each will reinforce the other to achieve planned objectives of wealth creation'. Mr Powell comments: 'a Church that is applying to itself objectives of wealth creation is a Church in flight from itself and, what is more, in flight from its founder'. But it is equally clear from his essays that Mr Powell would also object if the Church were to preach poverty as the aim of society as a whole. And Christian thinkers less controversial than Mr Powell would unite in a witness from many ages and social orders

that the Gospel is not about wealth or poverty in a material sense; is not primarily about social justice, but is about holy love; is not to be identified with the supremacy or revolt of any section of the community, as it has so tragically been identified in Northern Ireland or in Southern Africa, but is to be received with universal repentance and universal joy.

5. Yet if the message of Jesus was not primarily economic or political, it was not exclusively spiritual or personal. Jesus expected God to transform and rule all life, physical as well as spiritual, social as well as individual. Almost all his followers have had to go on living in the world, where their homes and jobs, often their voting rights and sometimes their positions of great responsibility, have all been spheres within which they have helped or hindered the coming of the Kingdom of God. Indeed there have been no easy answers, but to have said that the faith of Christians had no relevance at all to the problems faced by their societies would have been to condemn believers to schizophrenia. The point needs no further elaboration in a Church of England context. If evidence is needed of our Church's long tradition of concern for economic and political issues, it may be found in Philip Mairet's sketch of *The National Church and the Social Order* (1956), in Maurice Reckitt's *Maurice to Temple* (1947), and in John Oliver's *The Church and Social Order*, a study from 1918 to 1939 (1968). Many discussions of social problems have been held or sponsored by the Church Assembly or General Synod, particularly since the formation of a Social and Industrial Committee in 1923. And a recent reminder of the variety and vigour of the non-Anglican traditions in Britain has been provided by Daniel Jenkins in *The British: Their Identity and Their Religion* (1975).

6. How, then, is Christianity relevant? It is obviously impossible to summarise here the variety of answers given over the centuries. It must be enough to affirm that twentieth-century theology (both Catholic and Protestant) has come up with an answer: that the Gospel, while not itself economic or political, inspires thought and action which are in accord with certain axioms.

7. These are often called 'middle axioms', because they are midway between the Gospel and the detailed controversies and conflicts of the passing day. They are axioms which are important to Christians chiefly because they seem to be compatible with the revelation of God in Christ, and because for this reason they can be connected with many emphatic biblical teachings about justice and

righteousness (remembering that for Christians the Bible contains two Testaments). But these axioms may also be accepted by people who do not believe the Gospel. Jews, for example, can see them as the working out of the message of the law-givers and prophets of Ancient Israel; or Muslims as a modern application of the Koran. Believers in God who need not be Christians or Jews or Muslims can find the basis of these axioms in a 'natural order' or even in a 'natural law' evident without reference to any scriptures. Agnostics and atheists can ground them in humane but not religious ideals. This agreement between Christians and non-Christians makes it possible for Christians to join 'open' political parties or philanthropic movements, and to avoid a doctrinal test for admission into Christian Democratic Parties and similar 'Christian' movements.

8. Inevitably the axioms guiding social thought and action have been stated in many different ways. But recent Social Encyclicals have built up a body of teaching by the Popes, and among recent Anglican writers. T. S. Eliot (*The Idea of a Christian Society*, 1939), William Temple (*Christianity and Social Order*, 1942), D. L. Munby (*Christianity and Economic Problems*, 1956, etc.) and John F. Sleeman (*Economic Crisis: A Christian Perspective*, 1976) have all offered summaries which may be encapsulated together.

9. The resources of the earth, entrusted to man's care, are to be treated reverently and responsibly. Part of their use is to sustain human life, since man needs bread although he does not live by bread alone. The way in which they are used should provide creative and co-operative work in a group of the right size to be both human and efficient. It should also supply a material reward to all involved in the process, managers, administrators and workers alike – a 'just wage' meaning at least a payment on which the employee and his family can live with dignity. 'Wealth creation' is therefore a moral duty. But a 'just price' cannot be fixed by reference to the producer's needs only, for the earth's resources are to be distributed justly. By 'justice' here one means, basically, equality. Each consumer should count for one and no one for more than one whatever his or her class or race or nationality – unless it can be demonstrated that privileges given to one are ultimately for the good of all, for example by rewarding and thus encouraging scarce skills (see John Rawls, *A Theory of Justice*, 1971; criticised by Brian Barry in *The Liberal Theory of Justice*, 1973). It is also important for man to be free, the only tolerable constraints on his liberty being those which he accepts freely. In practice human freedom is 'freedom in a rocking boat'. Although denying him some chances, for example the chance to riot

or the freedom to starve at leisure, some constraints, such as the enforcement of the law or the discipline of work, enable man to take advantage of opportunities more important to his true welfare. High among the freedoms desired by believers in God must be the freedoms to worship and to obey God's law as this is discerned in prayer and free discussion.

10. It is a mark of the moral progress of the modern world that these axioms should be regarded so widely as platitudes. They are enshrined not only in the resolutions of a Vatican Council or a Lambeth Conference but also in the key documents of the United Nations. But Christians may legitimately claim that a special strength is given to these axioms when they are seen not only as humane ideals, and not only as attempts to restore a more natural order, and not only as reflections of the law of God for all men, but also as wisdom given by the Holy Spirit from the Father through the Son.

11. William Temple was right to say that Christianity is the most materialist of all the great religions, for it believes in the creation and glorification of all matter and all life by God. But that does not mean that Christians are materialists; they believe that God alone matters ultimately and lasts for ever, and their wish for the earth is that God's rule may come on it as in heaven.

12. To Christians, a reverent and responsible use of the earth's resources is encouraged supremely by the authority of Jesus, who, having worked as a carpenter, showed in his teaching of a supernatural Gospel such a tender regard for the beauty of nature and for the dignity of the world's everyday work. The processing and sharing of these resources should support human dignity, supremely because in Jesus God dignified human nature by using it to express himself. Distributive justice matters, supremely because Jesus was the fulfilment, not the denial, of the Old Testament–and therefore endorsed the insistence of Israel's prophets and law-givers that justice was the will of God. Equality and liberty for all are the foundations of a just society because of the truth of the fraternity of man under the Fatherhood of God, as revealed supremely in how Jesus taught, died and rose. Such a basis of social concern is, Christians think, more rock-like than is much other contemporary idealism, which may depend on short-term calculations or even on intellectual fashions. Here is, or ought to be, a foundation which can survive the crashing of many human hopes.

13. In its own life the Church shows, or fails to show, that it is built

on this rock. Often, and certainly in England, the Christian Church is put to the test because it is an organisation with a large staff, with a large membership, and with large assets including endowments which have to be invested. The way in which the Church treats its own staff, its own members and its own assets speaks to the world more loudly than anything that it may say in sermons or resolutions.

14. One of the major contributions of the Church to society lies in the sheer fact that it exists as an organisation, substantial and independent but not primarily political. This raises the hope that what it agrees to say and do in the social field – if it agrees to say or do anything – may contain elements of the impartial truth and activities which are genuinely useful. Much the same could be said about possible contributions by other non-political organisations such as charities or recreational clubs, but the Christian Church has more reasons than such bodies to make a major contribution. Indeed, Christians can find both general inspiration and practical examples in the communion of all those saints and sinners who have through many centuries been driven by Christian motives into the arena of economics and politics.

15. Members of the Church of England in particular may rejoice that this Church has fed Christians into work and public life in every generation since a date long before there was a United Kingdom or a single English kingdom. This heritage still lives in our time, when fairminded observers agree that the contribution made by Christians in social service, in charitable work and in moral leadership is far greater than the proportion of regular churchgoers in the population. To give one example, the Church of England has sponsored many chaplains within industry and has encouraged innumerable local discussions and activities responding to the challenges of an industrial society – as we are reminded by such a book as Margaret Kane's *Theology in an Industrial Society*, springing out of experience in N.E. England (1975). In its ability to mobilise idealism the Church of England can stand comparison with any of the political parties or with the trade union movement.

16. The Church enters the social field both through the teachings of its ordained or lay leaders and through the (probably more influential, although quieter) actions of its laity; and both teachings and actions are marked by certain characteristics whenever they are true to the spirit of Christianity. Christians worship the God of love. This means that they go among others as those who serve. They worship God as alone righteous. This means that they seek to be

genuinely humble both about their own moral claims and (even more difficult) about the moral claims of the groups to which they are loyal. They try never to be 'holier than thou'; and never to be unfairly partisan. They worship God who corrects and grants grace. This means that they are disposed, or at least self-disciplined, to accept correction through their fellow-Christians and their fellow-men; they try never to be pig-headed. But it also means that although deeply conscious of human frailty they rely on strength for the necessary work being given by God, day by day. Finally, Christians worship the ultimately triumphant God. This means that although deeply conscious of tragedy (does not their religion bear the cross as its sign?), they trust that what in their work has been in accordance with the will of God is not in vain, for in the end God wins. So they can sleep at nights. And so they can do the day's work, believing that even in tragedies which they cannot understand, God is working his purpose out; and confident that times of rapid and painful change (such as our own) can be among the birthpangs of the Kingdom of God. Such convictions have cleansed, strengthened and consoled countless Christians. They were never more needed than in England in 1976, a scene of mingled self-righteousness and gloom.

17. Thus the Church has a distinctive and significant contribution to make, although the goals which it pursues when serving society are shared by many others.

II BRITAIN IN PERSPECTIVE

18. The history of the Church includes many examples of Christians rising to new challenges thrown at them by their changing societies. New challenges are plentiful in Britain's economic and social crisis. But the first need is to understand that situation clearly.

19. In 1776, in *The Wealth of Nations*, George Adam Smith offered a pioneering analysis of the capitalist market place, in which through a network of detailed bargains consumers signalled what goods they wished to purchase, in exchange for what work, commodities or money. Despite the Marxist tone adopted by many vocal commentators, the vast majority of our fellow-countrymen two centuries later still believes in that kind of free market place as the most desirable arrangement in the inevitable circumstances. Its mechanism appears more efficient than any computer, let alone any Kremlin, yet conceivable. The main reason for this belief is that an economy operating mainly in this way has delivered the goods – almost certainly more successfully than would have been done at the command of Communist bureaucrats. The real value of wages and pensions in Britain since the war has, on average, about doubled. Our economic growth, around 2½ per cent per annum 1950–70, disappointed our ambitions but was still greater than anything seen when Britain was the 'workshop of the world' in the nineteenth century. Further credibility is given to capitalism by the greater progress of other non-Communist industrial nations.

20. But it is also true that over the last hundred years there has been a great, and usually a growing, belief in Britain that capitalism needs correction if it is to be acceptable. Young people have often said that they find capitalism disgusting; intellectuals, too, have tended to view the world of George Adam Smith as morally and aesthetically repulsive. (In 1876 prophetic articles appeared in the *Cornhill* by John Ruskin, and were collected the following year as *Unto This Last*.) Since, alas, moral and aesthetic considerations

have seldom governed human affairs when divorced from power, we may pass on to the fact that the working class have protested. In order to serve this class the State has played an ever larger role in the regulation of the economy, not only in Communist or Socialist countries but also in France and Italy and even in the three capitalist giants, the United States, West Germany and Japan. For Britain the symbolic date in determining the line taken by the State's intervention is the publication of *The General Theory of Employment, Interest and Money* by J. M. Keynes forty years ago.

21. This Cambridge economist dared to challenge the dogma that the lean years must follow the fat. He refused to accept a 'trade cycle' which meant a slump after a boom, as in the Hungry Forties, the great depression of 1873–96, or the misery of his own time (at one stage over 3 million unemployed). In his determination he articulated the conscience of many, including many Christians who did not pay enough attention to his work. But he also floated on the rising tide of working-class power, which was to bring a New Deal into Roosevelt's America and Labour into the government of Britain in 1945.

22. Whether for altruistic or for class reasons, full employment gradually became one of the most important goals of national policy; and only massive state intervention could enable this goal to be reached. At first as the suggestion by Keynes and a few fellow-theorists of a response to the emergency of the depression, then in wartime practice without much theory, and finally as the settled practice of the post-war years on the foundation of a sacrosanct theory, the State intervened to boost and direct economic growth along the channels it favoured, paying for this by greater taxation, by borrowing and by its control of the banks' credit-creation. The Keynesian formula that a nation could spend its way out of trouble worked brilliantly for many years. Over most of the period 1945–70, unemployment in Britain was almost always well below half a million in a labour force always above 20 millions. Keynes seemed to be the answer to Marx, for he had added the security of the workers to *The Wealth of Nations*, and Mr Macmillan was right both to affirm and to rejoice that the British people had never had it so good.

23. The British people did not only become more secure workers and more affluent consumers. They also constructed a Welfare State which set many new standards to other nations. And they took a pride in adding to it; during the 1960s the nation's expenditure on its Health Service doubled, as did the number of its full-time students.

Although some richer nations have now outstripped us in public services, the British educational system continues to attract pilgrims from abroad, as does the National Health Service. On a less elevated note, we should mention that the practical upshot of the nationalisation of the great public utilities in the 1940s was that the British people enjoyed more and better fuel and transport than would have been possible on strictly commercial considerations; the public sector of the economy was subsidised out of taxes drawn from the profits of the private sector. Nor should we forget the great burden of defence carried through years when the Soviet forces and missiles were reasonably thought to threaten Western Europe.

24. However, rising expectations were disappointed. The working class were still self-conscious despite some talk that the whole nation was becoming bourgeois as it settled down to watch TV. And they remained full of grievances. Indeed, throughout the 1960s resentment built up that the growing national prosperity, reflected so enticingly on TV, was not bringing greater advances to workers and their families. Colossal gains on the shady side of the financier's trade and in the property market (where fortunes were made out of planning permissions) had no equivalent for those who toiled with hand or brain. In 1959–69 the annual rise in manual workers' real earnings was, on average, only 2 per cent. There was no statutory minimum wage; agricultural labourers, manual workers employed by local authorities and hospitals, and many women were definitely paid too little. Some of the most socially valuable jobs – teachers or nurses, for examples – were poorly paid. The high salaries were often referred to as prizes in a rat race, and the highest were raised to such heights as to aggravate (partly in order to cope with tax). During the 1960s the poorest 10 per cent's share of total household income was approximately halved, and it was little consolation that the wealthiest 5 per cent also had a smaller share of the larger cake. Everywhere workers, even the affluent ones, continued to occupy a position distinctly inferior to 'management' or 'white-collar staff'. They were inferior in respect of educational opportunity, social status, the control of the conditions and rewards of work, job security, fringe benefits, effective medical treatment and pension rights. The cities did not have enough public money poured into making them enjoyable places to live. Rents of council houses and flats, although lower than the free market level, involved smaller subsidies than did the tax-privileged mortgages through which the middle classes bought their inflation-proof homes; and waiting lists were long. There were food subsidies, but more in the interests of the farmer than in those of the worker's family. The nationalisations of

the 1940s had brought little change for the average worker in the average company, and even in the nationalised industries the interests of the workers often seemed to them different from the board's.

25. All this resentment about the gap between 'we' and 'they' gave rise to a demand for more social equality. Fear bred a refusal to support the modernisation of industry; frustration boiled over into strikes. The bitterness should not be exaggerated: time lost due to industrial disputes in Britain 1955–64 was about a third what it was in the United States, and less than half what it was in West Germany. But conservative or disruptive practices in industry were symptoms of a malaise (see *Strikes*, edited by Ronald Preston, 1975). So was the feeling that the size of the pay packet was pretty well the only thing worth working for. With car workers as the pace setters (they had to be paid well to stand the boredom of the assembly line, and their products were the new gods of the people), and with miners as the shock troops (their conditions of work rightly commanded public sympathy), organised labour after years of relative quiet came to use strikes, or the threat of them, to clear the way to a fatter pay packet.

26. In 1974 the trade unions made clear their power over the country; the confrontation had reversed the fiasco of the 1926 General Strike. The Labour Government of 1974 was armed with a mandate by only about 40 per cent of the voters and about 30 per cent of the electorate, but its acceptance as the government probably reflected a more widespread feeling that Labour was the party most likely to find a broadly acceptable way out of the country's immediate difficulties. The current government programme of taxation (particularly penal taxation of property development for private gain), the protection of the lower paid, non-selective education, worker participation, pension reform, rate support grants, rent rebates, food subsidies and further nationalisation, with the control of key prices, seems likely to produce a more egalitarian Britain. If so, it will be a step comparable with the foundation of the Welfare State in the 1940s. Already it is estimated that every member of the working population receives the equivalent of £20 a week as a 'social wage' (the provision of new hospitals, schools and communications, the maintenance of old ones, and other social benefits and services). The pressure is on to raise this expenditure out of rates, taxes or borrowing by the local authority or the central government. In 1965–75 the number of employees in local government grew from 1½ to 2½

millions. In 1974–75 public expenditure grew by more than 40 per cent, almost a sixth of it (£7,500 million) from borrowing not taxation.

27. But still paradise is not in sight, for this progress, like every other in history, has carried a price. The day to which Keynes looked forward in a famous passage when economics would become unimportant has once again receded. The British people have found themselves paying the price of inflation, continuous and in the end almost uncontrollable – which Keynes had never anticipated. By the near-ruin of their currency they have been punished for demanding more than they have produced.

28. A 1944 White Paper on *Employment Policy* included a warning, but little attention was paid because wartime rationing and price controls had suppressed the inflationary effect of wartime employment. 1920 prices were not reached again until 1945. In 1950–70 the average annual rate of inflation was around 4 per cent. Wage restraint was included in the 1950s' bonfire of controls, and a 'pay pause' was not insisted on until 1961. In 1960–65 average wages rose by only 4½ per cent, and prices by 3½ per cent; in 1965–70, wages by 11 per cent and prices by 8 per cent. By 1973, however, the nominal value of wages and pensions in Britain had on average quadrupled since the war, and during 1974 it grew by almost a third. The trouble was that prices now caught up, whether pulled by consumers' demands or pushed by workers' costs. Many people did well out of this inflation; even in 1974 the average wage increase was about 10 per cent higher than the average price rise. But, sobered by the realisation that its actual production was stagnant or declining, the nation stared in the face the hyperinflation which destroys a society (Germany 1922–23, China 1945–48, Sukarno's Indonesia or Allende's Chile). With a slowness so agonising as often to appear suicidal, the British people accepted the need to bring inflation down to single figures, at which it might well be tolerable. Once more in 1975 national needs had to take precedence over free, collective bargaining over wages. Once more public spending had to be curbed and credit or subsidies to preserve or create jobs restricted. The freeze and the squeeze were back, with a million and a quarter unemployed, with the miseries of short-time working and bankruptcy, and with no realistic prospect of a quick reflation of the kind that had temporarily invigorated the economy in 1963, in 1967 and again in 1971. Even the goal of a 10 per cent inflation by the end of 1976 seemed distant. But by the end of 1975 there was the consolation that the rise in prices, although still horrifyingly over 25 per cent a year, had been cut by almost as much as the rise in wages.

29. Britain is still very far from being out of the wood; and if it has seen the wood of the total effects of inflation, it needs to see it more clearly. Despite the free lessons in economics distributed with the voting papers to the British electorate in 1974, despite recent world conferences and a flood of books (Sir Eric Roll's *The World after Keynes*, 1968, and Peter Donaldson's *Economics of the Real World*, 1973, stand out in the memory), the task still remains of fully alerting ourselves and any listeners to the international factors now causing inflation and other economic ills. These have prominently included the rise in commodity prices; the problem of balance of payments; the monetary problem; and the competition in exports.

30. The basic reason why *world commodity prices* rose by one and a half times in 1970–74 (although they fell back by a quarter in 1974–75) is the same reason why it was safe for the oil producers to quadruple their prices in the same period. We have now entered a world where the failure of a harvest in, say, Russia, or even a government's attempt to economise on the subsidy to grain stocks in, say, the United States, can bring the poorest food-importing countries such as India very close to famine – and can push up bread and meat prices in British shops to our dismay. The earth's resources are finite; even more limited are human abilities in exploiting those resources. The world's population doubled in 1940–70, and seems bound to double again in 1970–2000. Yet in recent years the world's agricultural production has either declined or risen by inadequate amounts, leaving 460 million people dangerously undernourished and many of the rest rightly or wrongly asking for more. The world's industrial production has grown more steadily – so steadily, indeed, that reports such as the Club of Rome's *Limits to Growth* (1972), or *Only One Earth* prepared for the United Nations by Barbara Ward and René Dubos (1972), warned that advancing industry including the industrialisation of agriculture was exhausting the earth's resources and polluting the environment, while a book such as E. J. Mishan's *The Costs of Economic Growth* (1967) showed that even an economist could ask whether it was worthwhile in terms of human happiness. But subsequent discussion – the 'second look at doom' – has tended to agree that the earth, if treated with due care, would turn out to be richer and tougher than the alarmists thought (see, for example, *Thinking about the Future* by the Science Policy Research Unit of Sussex University, 1973, and the Club of Rome's *Mankind at the Turning Point*, 1975). Discussion has also tended to agree that some economic, including industrial, growth remains essential if the population is not to sink completely into squalor and starvation. This was argued in Wilfred Beckermann's *In Defence of*

Economic Growth (1974), as in Bishop E. R. Wickham's booklet on *Growth and Inflation* (1975). The conservation of nature matters vitally – but it also matters that jobs should be found for the world's 200 million urban unemployed, and they cannot all be sent back to the countryside, where there is already underemployment of incalculable dimensions.

31. Whatever the long-term prospects, producers of food and of raw materials can certainly ask for and get higher prices from those able to pay, and the producers of oil can contribute both an example and a threat in the bargaining. The richer countries – that quarter of the world's population which still has three-quarters of the world's income – may complain that they are being held to ransom, like the British middle classes in reaction to the unions' wage demands; but as with the richer classes so with the richer countries – the medicine they had to swallow was not unlike the medicine which they had meted out to the poor in the days of their power, and morally speaking would seem more justifiable. Whatever our feelings, the cheap food, cheap raw materials and cheap energy which Britain enjoyed in the nineteenth century are now no more.

32. Another severe handicap to British prosperity has been the *balance of payments*. At various intervals in the late 1950s and the 1960s Chancellors of the Exchequer had to give the 'stop' sign to British economic growth all too soon after they had said 'go' – because growth resulted in more imports than the country could afford. Yet imports could not be penalised (save in a limited crisis such as 1964–66); they were needed too badly, and Britain depended too heavily on free trade, or on the EEC and GATT equivalents of it, for 'beggar my neighbour' policies to be sensible. The pound had to be devalued in 1949 and 1967 (from just over $4 to $2.40) and later, when more flexible rates of exchange became acceptable, had to be allowed to float downwards (to just over $2 at the end of 1975). The aim was to make British exports more competitive, although after a period the weakening of the pound always had the effect of making imports more expensive. Such problems would have spelt total disaster for a nation earning its living by trade had not sterling remained an international currency (a fact which itself added other burdens) and had not London successfully competed with New York as the leading centre of international finance and insurance (a fact which meant that the City often seemed more inclined to invest overseas than at home). In 1973, for example, the adverse balance in visible trade was £2,375 million, which was ten times the 1953 deficit (without adjustment for inflation) and was also roughly the cost of

the nation's food imports – but half this deficit was wiped out by the 'invisibles': interest, profits and dividends, private services and transfers. After the October 1973 war, although the new oil prices played the largest part in pushing the adverse balance in visible trade beyond the £4,000 million mark, Arab oil profits poured into the London Eurodollar market, into UK Treasury Bills, and into gilt-edged and equities quoted on the London Stock Exchange. Without these Arab investors we could not have afforded a public sector borrowing requirement likely to exceed £11,000 million in 1975–76.

33. The mighty United States proved unable to maintain the British level of employment, to balance its payments, or to keep its dollar convertible into gold; but it would seem that of all the world's major trading nations Britain has had the closest shave. These post-war troubles have not been allowed to interfere with Britain's domestic prosperity to anything like the extent to which the struggle to maintain the pound on the gold standard was allowed to swell British unemployment by preventing cost and price rises in 1925–31; but there has been an inescapable handicap, now universally admitted. The contrasting balances of West Germany and Japan (before the 1973 oil prices) were major factors in their spectacular successes.

34. The third international factor to be remembered when considering Britain's future is *the monetary problem*. In *Inflation: A World-wide Disaster* (1973), Irving S. Friedman of the World Bank raised the best argued of the many warning signs erected about that time against the growth of the world's money supply unmatched by growth in productivity. Obviously the entire structure of modern prosperity rests on the intricate, and to the inexpert eye scarcely real, network of credit manipulated by governments, banks and finance houses. It would be naive to think that every expenditure by a government should be paid for at once out of taxes, or that every pound lent by the banks should be matched by ten 10p pieces or by a pound's worth of wealth which one can already see and touch. It would also be wrong to think that there should be no inflation at all and therefore absolutely no growth in the money supply; periods when credit has been very difficult to come by have not been economically desirable years. Some inflation is acceptable, like (for most people) some alcohol. But just as there is a limit to an individual's consumption of alcohol, so money cannot be created and pumped into the economy *ad infinitum* without incurring the punishment of excessive inflation.

35. The Japanese themselves have had to limit their energies in

making yen, and the Federal Reserve Bank (no less) has had to sit tight on the dollar supply because its previous benevolence had been one of the causes of an inflation which had made a Republican president impose statutory controls on incomes and prices. To this day the United States accepts a dismal level of unemployment for the sake of monetary discipline. How much more has been the need of the United Kingdom not to print money, or to create credit, which would be too wildly out of keeping with real wealth! But the temptations of British governments to do just that, in a dash for growth, have also been greater. 1974 saw a general repentance, and the previous year's rate of growth in the money supply was halved although it had produced 5½ per cent growth. It began to seem almost as if money was no good because it was so easy to make, and there was some talk (for example, by the Editor of *The Times)* of a return to the gold standard.

36. Finally we come back to *industrial efficiency*. Since inflation is caused when consumers' or workers' demands outstrip producers' capacities, it is a law of life that disaster must come for any nation when too much paper money chases too few real goods – and too many imports are paid for by too few exports. A nation cannot feed itself on memories or demands.

37. It is now generally recognised that, on the whole, British industry has not adapted enough to the latest methods of efficiency. Partly this has been the fault of the workers – what with immobility, restrictive practices, wildcat strikes, demarcation disputes between unions, and other blocks and stoppages of production. Partly it has been due to the bosses' shortcomings in man-management, marketing, servicing, research and general enterprise. Partly it has been due to too frequent (and too little considered) changes in government policy and even in the machinery of government dealing with economic strategy; there has been no long-sustained national plan to indicate long-term targets. But mainly the fault seems to have been a lack of enthusiasm for innovation on the part of workers, managers and investors alike, despite government exhortations. For every worker in industry British firms have recently been investing only two-thirds as much as German firms, and only one-third as much as French firms; and this new investment has produced only one-third of the French level of new productivity. The cure for the British sickness would have been the regeneration of British industry, and the essence of this would have been not 'working harder' but lower unit costs. Mr Benn's estimate that British industry needs an extra £3,000 million a year in order to modernise its equipment has been

widely accepted. But in 1970–74, although the money supply swelled in the hope of giving birth to a boom, investment in capital equipment averaged just over 3 per cent of industrial production, less than half of what it had been in Britain in the 1960s and less than a quarter of what it was in Britain's main industrial competitors. Investment in property was more attractive. From 1974 onwards, when prices were being controlled for the sake of consumers, firms' profits were too low to encourage the vitally needed investment in renewal. All this meant that recently productivity per man hour in Britain has been little more than half the French and German levels and little more than a fifth of the American level. For this reason (among others) since 1963 French and German industrial production has been growing at about double our rate.

38. Britain still produces almost 5 per cent of the world's exports, no mean achievement. The trouble is that our competitors are getting better; as recently as 1960 the British share was over 8 per cent. In 1964–74 Britain's own imports of finished manufactures increased by 14 per cent, its exports of manufactures by only 6 per cent. As the careful, but perhaps too friendly, report by the Brookings Institute on *Britain's Economic Prospects* (1968) observed about this competition: 'Broadly speaking, Britain suffered smaller growth not so much because she fell short of other nations in any single source of growth as because each other country markedly excelled her in one or more of them' (p.11).

39. Less polite analysis became inevitable. In *The Collapse of British Power* (1972), Mr Correlli Barnett remorselessly pointed to warning signs going back to the 1870s. He argued that the imperial glory (or afterglow) had on the whole been a handicap since it had distracted Britain from its real interests in achieving industrial modernisation despite the immense costs of the two world wars. The danger that an underwater empire of oil could be a similar distraction from the need to keep up with foreigners industrially was driven home by the Hudson Institute in its 1974 report on *The United Kingdom in 1980*. These tough analysts argued that Britain, already competing with Italy and Ireland to be the poorest country in the EEC, was well placed to become the poorest in all Europe by the end of the 1970s – and to have a gross domestic product one-third the size of Japan's.

40. The pessimism of the Hudson Institute about Britain's prospects has been answered by much the same type of argument that was used to cheer up the Club of Rome in its contemplation of the

world scene. But it is clear that without a stronger economic base far less can be done than is desired to be done – and far less than ought to be done – for the stability of British democracy and for the improvement of the lot of the people; far less, too, for a generous role by Britain in a world moving fast towards famines and the consequent plagues and violence. Obviously Britain still belongs to the rich minority of mankind. Indeed, it is probably true to say that the British people were as a whole more prosperous in the mid-1970s than in almost any previous period, even if it was prosperity substantially financed by foreign lenders. Yet recent years have felt bleak to almost everyone in this country. The constant gloom of the news has matched our national mood. In addition to our practical problems, we have experienced the emotional traumas of disappointment and disillusionment. And we have no strong will to do better. In addition to knowing that our recent performance places us at the bottom of the league of the industrial nations, we fear what the future holds for this post-imperial island. And we have no clear plan.

41. The century opened with great hopes. As it draws to its close the four horsemen of the Apocalypse, once regarded as figures of a curiously worried past, seem near in our world, and even in our nation: the strong man on the white horse to whose dictatorship people submit in fear of worse, the troublemaker on the red horse who is given 'power to make men slaughter one another' in panic-induced conflicts, the announcer of hyperinflation on the black horse ('a whole day's wage for a quart of flour!'), and the bringer of disease and death on the sickly pale horse (Revelation 6. 1–8). In the 1970s that has often seemed a realistic answer to the challenge found in some manuscripts of Matthew's gospel: 'You know how to interpret the appearance of the sky; can you not interpret the signs of the times?' (16.3).

III THE RIGHT KIND OF UNITY

42. What can be done? Fortunately for us, the problem reduces itself at this moment to the simpler question: what can Christians, when gathered together, be expected to accept as the main outlines of what can and ought to be done in Britain now? The answer to be advocated here is *the right kind of unity for the right kind of growth*.

43. As the modern ecumenical movement reminds us in the ecclesiastical sphere, unity is a good which Christians feel morally obliged to seek unless there are compelling reasons of conscience against it. The same principle should govern a Christian approach to economics and politics. And it is an urgently relevant principle for the British in 1976. Perhaps the verse in the Bible which comments most aptly on our recent behaviour is the warning of Jesus that 'if a kingdom is divided against itself, that kingdom cannot stand' (Mark 3.4). Once one has looked into such an abyss, even survival at a reasonably comfortable level seems an attractive proposal, offering some hope of adventures later; and in recent years the British people have looked into the abyss. It has often seemed that the country was ungovernable because torn apart by a class struggle in which no class was willing to forget or to learn anything; that cohesion could not be restored except by a régime of Right or Left which would mean the end of democracy; that meanwhile inflation was the cancer which we encouraged as if we were all chain-smokers; and that this divided and bewildered Britain was incapable of maintaining anything like the present living standards of anything like its present population. (A widely noticed paperback of 1972, *A Blueprint for Survival* by the editors of the *Ecologist*, started from that assumption.) Therefore if 'unity for growth' is possible for Britain, it is not to be sneezed at.

44. *But it must be the right kind of unity, based on justice.* All too often 'unity' has been preached in a manner more attractive at the top than at the bottom of the pile. When a Conservative government is in power, the word 'unity' can easily seem to mean support for the

better off and a smile for the workers. In such a situation when spokesmen of the Church join in the cry for unity they deserve to be asked sharply whether they are seeking justice for the whole community – as they were asked by, for example, Bishop David Sheppard in his reflections on his inner London pastorate (*Built as a City*, 1974) or by the Rev. Dr Charles Elliott in his book reflecting his concerns as a Left-wing economist (*Inflation and the Compromised Church*, 1975). It is also the case that when a Labour government is in power those who are accused of sabotage tend to be people at cocktail parties, and it is less easy to ask the worker for a fair day's work (although the request has been made). The unity which we seek in our economic and political life must be agreement between all except extremist minorities about the long-term aims of our society.

45. It must be a unity which continues whatever government is in power. Disillusionment with party politics is now widespread. Mostly it is a priggish or ignorant reaction to the behaviour of politicians who have to wrestle with problems they did not dream up. But there is some validity in the feeling that the 'Westminster party game' is not very relevant to the real problems. People have in mind here the game of opposition with the suggestion that if only one was in office everything would be better; developing a fresh and radical programme which pleases the militants in the constituency parties; promising the moon to the electorate; when elected on these promises, being unable to carry them out; adopting instead some of the policies of the last government; adopting, in particular, unpopular economic policies; but reflating in time for the next election; and pleading throughout not only idealism but also consistency. If no political party has played this game, it is curious that so many people are under such an impression; and whether or not the sound of fiddling while Rome burns is an illusion, it is a fact that many people long for nobler and larger music. Britain remains a kingdom capable of being united for certain purposes.

46. If we ask 'what, then, divides it?' the answer in one word is *class*. The British tend to notice that their class divisions are less than they used to be, but foreign observers all comment that they are still very great. If the national unity is to transcend classes, the middle classes – from which the British churches are too largely drawn – need to be less snobbish, and less prone to adopt a morally superior tone when addressing the working class. For example, it is understandable that when the lights went out or the trains did not run businessmen and middle-class housewives complained that the

country was being held to ransom; but there is no evidence that, when given their opportunities, the middle classes have been behind-hand in the love of money or in the use of muscle (hospital doctors held the country to ransom in 1975). It would have been better for everyone if the frustrations of the working class had been recognised more effectively before they exploded into the strikes of 1972. But in their turn the working class – with whose complaints many church leaders sympathise – need to be fixed less firmly in the memories of the 1920s, and less censorious about the creators of wealth. For example, it is perhaps understandable that stockbrokers should be thought to lead idle and non-productive lives in comparison with labourers; the City of London has for long been a favourite target of critics, with its turtle soup, its dances of bulls and bears, and its sinister connections with gnomes and sheikhs. But on the figures it is hard to see how, without the City and what it represented in the way of wealth-creation, the British people could have been fed (just as it is hard to see how, without the Church Commissioners' investments in shares and property, now yielding £34 million a year, the clergy of the Church of England and their families could have been fed). The wiping out of the growth of twenty years, which occurred on the Stock Exchange 1973–4 and which has now been partly rectified, did nobody any good. The willingness of savers to save and invest in 1974–5 surprised everyone, but saved the economy. Now we need an understanding that a prosperous future cannot be built without labour – or without capital.

47. If the classes are to understand each other better, their members must meet each other more. Of course this already goes on in many places where people dress sufficiently alike and have enough in common not to feel 'we' and 'they' all the time – from those who wear jeans in discos to those who wear suits in the Town Hall. There are, indeed, many signs that intelligent people are feeling about snobbery (or its inverse) as they do about colour prejudice. But emotions between classes spring from contrasts between income groups, and in the years to come a high priority will have to be given to meetings which can result in agreements between sectional interests.

48. It is for discussion whether the National Economic Development Council (for example) does not need to be strengthened, with more frequent and substantial meetings and a larger staff, to sustain the importance of this exchange of views between the government of the day, the TUC and the CBI; it is, after all, far more important than the House of Lords. Already the discussion has begun about the

representation of workers on the supervisory boards or advisory councils of companies – a development of industrial democracy where Britain is sadly behind Sweden and almost all its European partners. To this discussion, the booklets on *Work in Britain Today* (1969) and *Power Sharing in Industry* (1975) are valuable contributions from the Industrial Committee of the Church of England's Board for Social Responsibility.

49. A body such as the Church cannot be expected to arbitrate in class or other sectional conflicts – or to anticipate the details of agreements to be reached when the parties in dispute have met with the intention of agreeing, and when the experts have debated each other's factual arguments. But it seems legitimate, if a trifle risky, to point to questions which demand fresh and constructive thinking.

50. *We need to revise the aims of industry.* It has often been said that basic attitudes on both sides are still all too often those which were natural in the age of *laissez faire*; it has even been said that in the car industry (for one) they are the attitudes of trench warfare. Whether the workers' representatives are to have places on supervisory boards or are to be non-executive directors, and whether or not they are to have parity with shareholders in deciding the crucial issues, they will have to be guided by a bigger interest than the battle for wages. Whether or not the managers are to be responsible in terms of power and law to the workers as well as to the shareholders or to a nationalised industry's Board, they will have to be inspired by a broader ambition than the growth of sales. Wages are important, and sales make them possible. But what makes workers involved and satisfied in addition to paper money? And what would make customers happier than the goods now being sold? And what is the optimum size for the work-group and for the firm? In response to such questions we need a constant and detailed effort to make work at every level a support to human dignity, not its destruction – and to put work at every level in the context of a moral vision of service to the nation and the world. The great capitalist 'miracles' of industrial growth in North America, West Germany, France and Japan depended for their take-off on a supply of first-generation industrial labour, glad to escape into the factories from the poverty of the immigrant ghettos, the Russian colonies, the declining farms or the war-devastated cities Britain may have denied itself the chance of developing such a capitalist economy when it restricted immigration from the Commonwealth countries; and certainly today it is unrealistic to expect that the British will exactly copy the American, German or Japanese attitudes, all of which spring from

those nations' histories. But now British workers and managers have an opportunity to show really mature attitudes to industrialism, nationalising and humanising the aims of industry. Desirable attitudes are found plentifully in the new sciences of management and industrial relations. They are practised often. But it is generally held that they are not yet practised enough – and that Christians in industry have a contribution to make.

51. *We also need to restate the aim of full employment.* This aim needs to be reaffirmed. Suggestions to the contrary are almost universally, and rightly, regarded as immoral. They also depend on the politically ignorant idea that the working class (still usually reckoned to be the majority of the British electorate) would accept another aim, and on the economically ignorant idea that massive unemployment would be bound to produce an inflation-free recovery. If it were to be widely believed that any government had abandoned this aim, the workers' acceptance of that government's incomes policy would not be willing; and if it was not willing, it would not be lasting. But recent developments stress the importance of restating the aim. Full employment in Britain depends on Britain's capacity to export, since the world does not owe this island a living. Employment in the service industries cannot grow safely unless a proper provision is made for manufacturing (which at present employs about half our labour force, but the proportion has been declining). It is for discussion whether the Selective Employment Tax was not, after all, a sensible one. And in the opinion of many shrewd observers it needs to be acknowledged – as the last resort, by revising unemployment benefits – that the labour force must be more willing than it has been to move from job to job and from place to place as the demands of a modern economy dictate. Generous retraining and resettlement grants, with the all-important provision of housing near the new work, must be seen as essential parts of modernisation, however complex the problems may be. These points demand discussion within the setting of the battle for full employment.

52. Connected with this is *the question of the place of private business in a mixed economy*. It is mythology that these businesses usually consist of little but rugged men, with their families and a few friends, competing to serve their neighbours more cheaply. A large slice of the private sector in Britain is owned by multinational corporations whose assets exceed those of many of the proud States meeting in the General Assembly of the United Nations. It is also mythology that the profits made by private businesses are evils to be tolerated only because of the taxes that can be levied on them.

Recent speeches by Mrs Thatcher and Sir Keith Joseph have rendered a public service by challenging the public as to what it does think about the private enterprise on which it relies so heavily. But in the necessary reassessment, the nation needs to acknowledge (forgetting other myths) how unlikely it is that sufficient investment in private businesses will be generated by private investors. Already pension funds and insurance companies play massive, often dominant, parts on the Stock Exchange; and the recent difficulties of Rolls Royce, Burmah Oil, British Leyland and Chrysler have been forcible reminders that ducks which most people reckoned to be strong cannot cross the road nowadays without the assistance of the State, given reluctantly in order to save jobs. The establishment of the National Enterprise Board will, it is to be hoped, produce a really enterprising policy of State participation in industrial renewal.

53. Another question is *the place of trade unions in a society which values freedom under the law.* It is mythology to think that these unions usually consist of cloth-capped, horny-handed sons of toil bravely defying wicked employers in order that their children may not starve. The unionised workers were remarkably successful until 1975 in avoiding the consequences of inflation, and many of their energies have been bent on preserving or increasing differentials between workers. It is also mythology that unions must be opposed to efficiency; the American and EEC experiences in recent years have shown that. Mr Heath's administration did well by the nation when it attempted to do something about the problems spotlit by the Donovan Report and the 1969 White Paper *In Place of Strife.* They tried to enforce cooling-off periods before many strikes, to curb unofficial strikes, to draw up a code of practice to guide management and unions alike, and to bring the unions more firmly under the courts in the last resort. The fact that they failed does not mean that all these objectives can safely be forgotten. But it was less wise to attempt to enforce a law which the unions had announced they would ignore, or even to legislate when the unions refused to be consulted. A happier climate will, it is to be hoped, lead to a bold policy of self-criticism by the unions.

54. In an age of inflation it is inevitable that a 'social contract' between government and trade unions should lead to *a prices policy.* It is never practical to fix all prices; not even Communist régimes achieve that, and what they do achieve in fixing most prices is scarcely an advertisement for the efficient supply of goods in a sophisticated economy. Nor is it practical to fix any prices so low that the producers or sellers have an inadequate profit margin.

Competition remains the best regulator (with anti-monopoly laws). But recent British experience has surprised the sceptics by showing that it is possible to monitor key prices and to guide them with a view to the national interest. Evidently the medieval and Tudor tradition of price-control based on a religious ethic is not totally irrelevant.

55. There remains the question of an incomes policy. Mr Aubrey Jones in *The New Inflation* (1973) told the story of the agonies of successive governments and successive agencies following the Statement of Intent agreed upon by the government with representatives of the trade unions and the employers in 1964. The intent to achieve real, instead of inflationary, wage rises remains at the centre of any realistic plan for our people's economic progress, and the acceptance of the £6 a week limit in 1975 holds out more hope than Mr Jones could allow himself that the many fine words are at length leading to an effective plan. But the Draconian nature of the 1975 'plan to save the nation', voluntarily accepted, cannot be made permanent. There seems no alternative to working out methods by which a flat rate plus a percentage of income plus rewards for productivity plus recognition of changing differentials can be recommended by an authority more acceptable than the government alone (for the government is Britain's largest employer), the employers alone, or the unions alone (for both employers and unions will take long to live down their past irresponsibility). And as the Liberals (alone) have always insisted, there is no alternative to fining or otherwise punishing any breach of this policy – although obviously it is best for the policy to be 'voluntary' in the sense that sanctions lie dormant.

56. Clearly the question of *what* flat rate and percentage of income are to be allowed must be related to national productivity, and the question of what differences in needed skills or outputs are to be acknowledged financially must be resolved after a national stocktaking (which the current Royal Commission on incomes has begun, and which need not be begun afresh every year). Clearly, too, a more rational method of wage-bargaining will have to reduce the present fragmentation in the British trade union movement, and will have to restrict the number of times when new bargains can be struck between employers and employees either nationally or locally. And clearly many other daunting problems will have to be faced. But to suggest that the nation cannot summon up the moral and intellectual effort involved in agreeing on the principles behind just wages in the 1970s is to suggest that the nation cannot survive

in a world where neither inflation nor the periodic readjustment of relativities can be completely avoided. The Church and every other public-spirited group have a clear duty to stimulate this debate and to set an example by real responsibility for the pay of their own staffs.

IV THE RIGHT KIND OF GROWTH

57. It is the general teaching of the Bible that God wants the earth to be fruitful under man's stewardship; Adam is meant to make the garden grow. Some Christians have a Franciscan-type vocation to be poor or 'zero-growth' people in their own lives, just as some have a vocation to be pacifists consistently rejecting arms; and that witness is invaluable. And plainly other Christians more intent on economic growth have no special qualifications to give advice in a field where so many highly trained politicians, civil servants, financiers and business and union chiefs (and even academics) have so far so largely failed. The Bible does not contain a better National Plan than the one unveiled in 1965, abandoned in 1966, and never replaced. But it seems possible for the Church to endorse some conclusions of recent discussions, and to commend these conclusions enthusiastically to the whole nation.

58. *Provided that it does not damage the environment, the workers or the community, economic growth is a good thing because it enables us to pay for what we want.* Most Christians would agree that there can be a 'just war', a war waged for certain reasons and within certain limits. So it is with the idea of a 'just growth'. The right reason for growth is to increase the real welfare of the whole people, and the proper limit to growth is set by the nature which (Christians would add: by the God who) makes economic growth possible. 'Just' growth does not mean destroying the happiness of the majority in order to multiply the comfort or ostentation of an élite; nor does it mean wrecking our irreplaceable planet. What does it mean, then? What is democratic growth? What is sustainable growth? The necessary rethinking of the 1970s has scarcely begun within the terms set by our newly aroused social conscience and our new knowledge of sociology and ecology. A book such as J. K. Galbraith's *Economics and the Public Purpose* (1974) is an American economist's prophecy to the once carelessly affluent society of Western capitalism, and a group of economists commissioned by the British Council of Churches will present a report during 1976.

On the question of how much raw material and energy the earth may be expected to produce without overstraining itself, some light is thrown by the World Council of Churches' *Report on Nuclear Energy* (1975). Over the next few years we may hope for more light from research and discussions being sponsored by the United Nations. A stock-taking of the creation is in process, for the first time in history.

59. *Britain in particular needs economic growth for its welfare, for some down-to-earth reasons.* It needs *to grow more of its food* in a world where only shortages are certain to grow. It would benefit if it could improve on its present position where about half its food supply depends on imports (feeding stuffs for animals, fertilisers for crops, and oil for energy, as well as imported food). This is not a simple matter: it means encouraging British farmers without breaking EEC rules; it means reducing imports without ruining Third World farmers; it means educating British consumers without a Communist dictatorship. But the experts say that much can be done, and a Church with a great presence in the countryside will naturally take an interest.

60. However, Britain also needs more *industrial growth* – and not only in order to support its agriculture. This country is, and intends to remain, a democracy. This means that its rulers must, broadly speaking, obey its people's wishes. Realistically neither the middle nor the working class can be expected to accept a voluntary drop in their material living standards, or to renounce their ambitions, in order that reduced resources may enrich the other class; and in practice, whatever the morality of the situation may be, the British electorate is not likely to wish for seriously reduced standards in order that British national interests may be subjected to the interests of poorer (or richer) countries. Since roughly speaking no one is prepared to give up anything much, 'growth' remains the only way by which a democracy can do new things which are, either for material or for moral reasons, desirable. And in the special circumstances of Britain, industrial growth is specially desirable. On the one hand, Britain's laws against pollution by industry are a model to the world, and could be tightened further if the country could afford the added costs to industry. On the other hand, as successive Chancellors of the Exchequer have agreed, increased production by more modern methods is for Britain the only escape from the five unwelcome problems – the inflationary effect of maintaining full employment and the Welfare State on the basis of inadequate growth, the rise in the price of raw materials, the need to balance

imports with exports, the need to match the rise in the money supply with actual wealth, and the need to compete industrially if Britain is not to be reduced to importing manufactures on an ever-growing scale. For an exporting industrial nation, life is not cricket: it is a race. Many commentators have also drawn attention to the shameful greed and folly of this country's recent attitude, which was that consumer goods and social services could be enjoyed without being earned. The earliest surviving Christian document contains relevant teaching: 'Let it be your ambition . . . to work . . . so that you may command the respect of those outside your own number, and at the same time may never be in want' (I Thessalonians 4. 11, 12).

61. *If we want a 'just' growth, then we should go all out for it.* If we are serious about rejecting random growth which would destroy the environment and dehumanise the workers, it follows that far more attention needs to be paid to the drastic reduction of pollution and waste, to monitoring the supply of raw materials, to the discovery of substitutes where needed, to the ecology of agricultural expansion, and to humanising the conditions of industrial work in consultation with workers – all highly technical subjects. If we are serious about wanting to compete industrially, it follows that the confidence and energy of our financial and business leaders need to be aroused by something more than words; and that the attention of the trade union movement from top to bottom needs to be switched from fatter pay packets to real improvements, and from the defence of jobs as they are to the discovery of a viable economy. And the enthusiasm of a new generation needs to be directed into science, engineering, technology and industrial management. In all these subjects Britain's educational resources are at present either inadequate or under-used by students. The belief inspiring the Church to support all these hard-headed moves – so unlike the general impression of the Church's remoteness, nostalgia and sentimentality – should be the conviction that the Creator has entrusted to us the resources of the earth (and the talents of hand and brain) with the intention that we should use them with the beauty of efficiency. This belief is hypocrisy, however, unless there is a continuous search for efficiency in church life. The present reorganisation of the parishes is a beginning.

62. *Perhaps more than we deserve, we shall have a chance in the 1980s; and that chance must not be frittered away.* Britain's opportunity in the first industrial revolution came because of its new world market, because of its coal, because of its people's

inventiveness and patience, and because of the international standing of its currency. Now Britain is given a last chance to take advantage of the second industrial revolution, based on automation and other production methods which use scientific knowledge and computers rather than hands. We have a new market in the EEC, supplemented by the trading links which survive from a previous era. In the 1975 referendum the British people had the realism to embark on a course which must end in the United States of Europe, to the benefit of everyone concerned. Most of Britain's problems are now shared with other European peoples; so are most of Britain's hopes. We have new sources of energy – the ocean bed sources which are expensive to exploit (meaning that we can neither expect nor want much of a fall in the price of oil), and nuclear power (but power from fission methods will require great attention to safety, and the technology for the safer fusion system has not yet been developed). At least these new sources are under our control, and will free us from the balance of payments prison. We have a new mood of realism as the gravity of our crisis has been brought home. And a new agreement seems to be emerging to secure an international monetary order (exchanges will be flexible within limits to be supported by central banks, and gold is not necessary). With these hopeful signs, almost all the experts are agreed that a steady industrial growth, accompanied by a tolerable balance of payments, is now possible technically, *if there is the will.* When considering this possibility, Christians will recall that it took the Creator millions of years to make the oil and the gas which, it is now hoped, can fuel Britain for perhaps a century until safe, cheap and abundant nuclear power is available. Christians will also recall that the Creator is responsible for all the other natural resources and human skills and hopes which make up Britain's chance.

63. *Creative investment should be encouraged from all sources, but a firm's obligations to its shareholders should be considered alongside its obligations to its employees and to the public.* If it is true that in the present state of British industry more fiscal incentives are needed to stimulate creative investment by individuals, companies and funds, then priority should be given to them. It has been suggested that the tax privileges to investors should amount to treating the whole of Britain, not merely its poorer regions, as a 'development area' for a period. If it is true that in the present state of the capital market (due partly to the taxes which the State extracts from people previously able to save and invest large sums) large investments by the State are needed, taxpayers must accept a large part of the outlay. If it is desirable that both private investors

and the State should take a closer interest in the day-to-day efficiency of industry, arrangements should be made. It is widely agreed that those who provide the finance ought not to need take-overs and asset-stripping in order to be 'company doctors' when a company is ill; and that the State needs planning agreements with the key firms, on the French model. But if managers, workers and consumers are also to be treated fairly, all this emphasises the importance of a drastic reform of company law, still basically what it was made in 1862. At present a company is said at law to be run by its directors for the benefit of its shareholders, but its practice tends to be determined by what its managers decide after (often superficial) contacts with shop stewards, salesmen and civil servants. In *The Responsible Company* (1961) an Anglican businessman, Mr George Goyder, urged that a firm's obligations and accountability should be defined, and the participation of Anglicans in later discussions leading to a code of practice for directors is shown by Mr Kenneth Adam's booklet on *Ethical Choice and Business Responsibility* (1975).

64. *Allocating the first-fruits of growth to strengthen producers, not to fatten consumers, means a change in the national mood.* A democracy is not likely to accept voluntarily a sizeable drop in its standards of living (it may choose that unconsciously, as indeed Britain has been doing). But it is not necessary for a democracy to be deceived by the advertisers' lie that happiness rests on a mountain of flashy, expensive and ephemeral consumer goods. The 'consumer movement', now backed officially, is helping us to be more discriminating in our purchases. Many young people do not believe that the best things in life can be advertised (see, for example, Kenneth Leech, *Youthquake,* 1973). They might warm to John Ruskin's words of 1876: 'Many joys may be given to men which cannot be bought for gold, and many fidelities found in them which cannot be rewarded with it . . . Political economists will do well some day to take heed of it, though they cannot take its measure' (*Unto This Last,* pp. 2-3). Fortunately, too, the Christian tradition of asceticism has always been a pressure encouraging depth and simplicity of life. Among recent contributions by leaders of the Church of England making this ancient tradition relevant and urgent may be mentioned Bishop Hugh Montefiore's work *(Can Man Survive?*, 1969, etc.), Bishop John Taylor's book *Enough is Enough* (1975), Sir John Lawrence's *Take Hold of Change* (1975), and the call to the nation by the Archbishops of Canterbury and York (1975). Above all, the parochial clergy have set an example by accepting austere incomes with few complaints.

65. But much more detailed work needs to be done before an alternative style of life, which might be called a 'just consumerism', can be seen as practical and attractive by our people. For this is a people which knows that its prized standards of living have depended on competition in industry and trade and must depend in the future on more, not less, use of science. If the recently dominant cult of rapidly obsolescent consumer goods is to be rejected, so also is any back-to-nature fantasy. What most of us in Britain want is the priority of the happiness and spiritual vitality of the individual and the family, plus the ordering of our lives so that we live more harmoniously with nature and with each other, plus an adequate supply of the goods which support the good life (for example, housing or nourishment or medicine or education or the arts or sport, in every case needing money). Most of us would reckon that such a quality of life is within Britain's grasp, and that our present time of troubles will have been worth enduring if it gives birth to a civilisation so humane, and so truly rich, worthy of a very great past.

66. *In the near future, if there is to be more investment in the renewal of industry the nation must accept a smaller increase in pay than is immediately popular.* It may well be that in the 1980s the real value of workers' wages will safely rise by no more than the disappointing average of the 1960s. And it may well be that such wages will be accepted because they will be seen to belong to a national plan involving a fair deal for all (including restraint on salaries and dividends) and a realistic hope for the future. One who fought hard for the advance of the working class, G. D. H. Cole, wrote at the end of his study of *The Post-War Condition of Britain* (1956): 'The urgent need for the time being is to achieve higher all-round productivity and to guide a high proportion of the increase into investment until the productive structure has been thoroughly re-equipped.' That challenge has only been intensified by the last twenty years.

67. In the creative period of Britain's first industrial revolution, investment in production was given priority over the wishes of consumers. The same was true of the creative periods in the Communist revolutions in Russia and China. Growth was achieved in all three advances at an appalling price in terms of human happiness or liberty, and we must all hope that no such price need be paid by Britain in what remains of the twentieth century. But some price must be paid if people wish to retain, let alone increase, the present wealth underpinning British life. Some more words which Ruskin

wrote amid another recession, a hundred years ago, deserve to be remembered. 'Luxury is indeed possible in the future – innocent and exquisite; luxury for all, and by the help of all; but luxury at present can be enjoyed only by the ignorant' (*Unto This Last,* p. 173).

68. *The growth of real wealth in Britain must be set in the context of a new economic order for the world.* According to the Christian tradition, riches can be earned morally by the willingness to share them with the poor. The oil-producing States, mainly Muslim, now set an example in this; 1.8 per cent of their gross national product is given in official aid to the developing nations, as compared with under 0.4 per cent in Britain. But aid is not enough. By the phrase 'new economic order' we should mean specifically the acceptance of the proposals made by the developing nations in 1974–75. These proposals involve (1) more aid with fewer strings – 0.7 per cent of g.n.p. remains the UN recommendation; (2) more loans on better terms; (3) higher prices for raw materials in order to compensate for dearer energy and imported equipment or manufactures; (4) stable commodity prices after negotiations where producers' associations would speak; (5) tariff privileges along the lines of the EEC's recent Lomé Convention – a monument of enlightened statesmanship; (6) a careful regard to the supply of raw materials before developing synthetic substitutes; (7) special 'drawing rights' with the International Monetary Fund in order to ease the balance of payments; (8) some form of control by the United Nations of those activities of multinational corporations which at present exploit the poorer countries; (9) patent privileges to help industrialisation, with assistance in starting shipping lines and insurance services; and (10) the development of trade *between* developing nations. These are not the new ten commandments, but these things are what the world's poor now want from us, and it should be our ambition to be able to say yes.

69. Through its support of Christian Aid and in many other ways, the Church has been foremost in campaigning on behalf of the world's poor. Any support now given by the Church to the rescue of Britain from economic disaster must keep in view this nation's manifold responsibilities and opportunities in world development. Industrial renewal leading to a substantial growth in the British economy during the 1980s could help to make the world a safer and happier place during the twenty-first century.

V SUMMARY

70. Although we should not look for specifically Christian economics or politics, we should be faithful to the long tradition of Christian involvement in Britain's problems in the service of justice, freedom and other ideals which non-Christians, too, can accept. Indeed, in pursuing these goals the Church has a distinctive and significant contribution to make. The first task of Christians responding to Britain's present economic crisis is therefore to reach an objective understanding of its causes – the inflationary effects of wage rises; the revolution in commodity prices; the handicaps imposed on industrial growth by the dangers of excessive imports and an excessive money supply; the inefficiency of out-of-date machinery and attitudes.

71. To meet these challenges, Britain needs the right kind of unity. This means a unity founded on justice in our society and in particular on a greater reconciliation between classes. We need to restate realistically what are the aims of individual firms, and what is our nation's aim in maintaining full employment; what are the places of trade unions and private businesses and what are the right levels of prices and wages, as indicated in an agreed national plan.

72. Britain also needs the right kind of growth. This means growth which increases the real welfare of the whole people and which uses the earth's resources responsibly. If we want such growth, we should go all out for renewal and expansion even if it means accepting disappointing rises in wages, salaries and dividends. So we can earn our living as an industrial, exporting nation, and make our contribution to the new economic order needed in the world.

QUESTIONS FOR DISCUSSION

Suggestions for groups using this pamphlet

1. Do you agree that 'we need not look for specifically Christian economics or politics'?

2. Which of the 'axioms' on which Christians and others can unite seem to you most relevant to Britain now?

3. Where do you think the Church's contribution to society is currently lacking?

4. Do you agree that an economy operating mainly as a free market place has largely 'delivered the goods' for Britain?

5. What do you reckon to be the main causes of Britain's current social revolution?

6. What do you think matters most in causing Britain's inflation?

7. Is 'the right kind of unity for the right kind of growth' the right kind of aim for you?

8. What would you say a reconciliation between the classes involves?

9. Do you consider a long-term incomes policy possible?

10. What kind of economic growth, if any, do you regard as desirable?

11. Does this paper say enough about agriculture?

12. In your experience, is this paper right to claim that new attitudes are needed in industry?

13. In your opinion, is this paper sufficiently Christian in its advocacy of a 'just growth' in the richer countries, and even a 'just consumerism'?

14. What action do you intend to take after this discussion?